Dedicated to Niki, Dimitris, Lelis

Dedicated to my wonderfully patient hus
Dora and her family, our parents Elisavet

Copyright © 2020 Elisavet Arkolaki, Charikleia Arkolaki

Translated into French by Sophie Troff.

For permission requests and supplementary teaching material, please write to the publisher at liza@maltamum.com www.maltamum.com

ISBN 9798677101281

Today I felt like painting the sea. We took our brushes, watercolors, art pads, and a glass of water and sat on the veranda to paint. A little blue, a little yellow, a little brown and look, that's how it all started.

Aujourd'hui, j'ai eu envie de peindre la mer. Nous avons pris les pinceaux, aquarelles, carnets de dessin et un verre d'eau, et nous nous sommes installées sur la terrasse pour peindre. Un peu de bleu, de jaune, de marron, et regardez, c'est ainsi que tout a commencé.

I was reminded of the summer vacations we took, to the place where my mother grew up, and I added some rocks to the landscape. Purple for the sparse clouds and this green for the hill seem to be a great match.

Cela m'a rappelé nos vacances d'été à l'endroit où ma mère a grandi, et j'ai ajouté quelques rochers au paysage. Le mauve des nuages clairsemés et le vert de la colline vont très bien ensemble.

We'd go to the sea every morning and play there for hours. All the colors of summer were imprinted on our swimsuits. Intense yellow, intense blue, and intense orange.

On allait à la mer tous les matins et on jouait pendant des heures. Toutes les couleurs de l'été étaient imprimées sur nos maillots de bain. Jaune vif, bleu vif et orange vif.

I also remembered the small church. It was on the hill. Our grandmother would sometimes take us there before we returned home for lunch. I'll mix a little brown, a little yellow, and a little green.

Je me suis souvenu aussi de la petite chapelle sur la colline. Notre grand-mère nous y emmenait parfois avant de rentrer déjeuner à la maison. Je vais mélanger un peu de marron, de jaune et de vert.

On the way back we often picked wildflowers to arrange them in a vase. I think orange, purple and green are very suitable here.

Sur le chemin du retour, on cueillait des fleurs sauvages pour les mettre dans un vase. Je trouve que l'orange, le violet et le vert font très jolis ici.

When we got home, and after we had eaten our food, she offered us the most delicious fruit. Green for the fig, orange for the apricot, and red for the peach.

Une fois à la maison, après avoir fini notre assiette, elle nous offrait les fruits les plus délicieux. Vert pour la figue, orange pour l'abricot et rouge pour la pêche.

Grandma also had a cat. We played so many different games inside and outside, running after her in the narrow dead-end street. It was, indeed, Happiness Street! Her colors were white, brown, and bright green.

Grand-mère avait aussi une chatte. Nous avons joué à tant de jeux dans la maison et dehors, courant après elle dans cette impasse étroite. C'était vraiment la rue du Bonheur ! La chatte était de couleur blanche, marron et vert clair.

In the afternoons we used to take a stroll down the beach again. I'll mix brown, green, and white for the trail.

L'après-midi, on retournait souvent nous promener vers la plage. Je vais mélanger le marron, le vert et le blanc pour le chemin.

How beautiful those sunsets were!
We take a whole trip back in time
with a little purple, yellow, and brown.

Comme les couchers de soleil étaient
beaux ! Nous allons remonter le temps
avec un peu de violet, de jaune et de
marron.

We'd bring our food with us,
lay the mat down on the sand
and eat under the starry sky.
Dark yellow, dark blue, and a
dash of red, and we're there
again.

On emportait de la nourriture,
étalait la natte sur le sable
et mangeait sous le ciel étoilé.
Jaune sombre, bleu foncé,
une touche de rouge, et nous
y sommes à nouveau.

I remember the landscape changed dramatically when autumn came. We knew then that it was time to leave.
Mom was coming.
The colors are getting really dark now, intense blue, deep green.

Je me souviens que le paysage changeait de façon spectaculaire à l'automne. On savait qu'il était temps de partir, que maman allait venir. Les couleurs s'assombrissent maintenant, bleu intense et vert foncé.

But look at the composition,
how it changes again, and how
the hazy colors are making
room for other happier ones.
Mom also brought along with
her white, pink, and gold,
and a promise that yes,
we'd leave, but we would come
back again.

Mais regardez comme la
composition change à nouveau,
et comment les couleurs
brumeuses font place à des
teintes plus gaies. Maman a
apporté le blanc, le rose et l'or
et la promesse que oui, même si
nous partions, nous reviendrions
un jour.

Dear Child,

Every summer has a story. This is a story inspired by my own childhood, and my sister's watercolors. Ask an adult to help you write down the words and draw the images of your own summer story, and send me an email at liza@maltamum.com I promise, I'll write back to you.

Dear Grown-up,

If you feel this book adds value to children's lives, please leave an honest review on Amazon or Goodreads. A shout-out on social media and a tag #HappinessStreet would also be nothing short of amazing. Your review will help others discover the book and encourage me to keep on writing. Visit eepurl.com/dvnij9 for free activities, printables and more.

Forever grateful, thank you!

All my best,
Elisavet Arkolaki

Made in the USA
Las Vegas, NV
27 November 2023

81614255R00019